TRINITY
COLLEGE LONDON PRESS

CW00429411

GRADE

04
VOCALS

Published by
Trinity College London Press Ltd
trinitycollege.com

Registered in England
Company no. 09726123

Photography by Zute Lightfoot, lightfootphoto.com

Printed in England by Caligraving Ltd

Parental and Teacher Guidance:

The songs in Trinity's Rock & Pop syllabus have been arranged
to represent the artists' original recordings as closely and
authentically as possible. Popular music frequently deals with
subject matter that some may find offensive or challenging.
It is possible that the songs may include material that some
might find unsuitable for use with younger learners.

We recommend that parents and teachers exercise their own
judgement to satisfy themselves that the lyrics of selected
songs are appropriate for the students concerned. As you
will be aware, there is no requirement that all songs in this
syllabus must be learned. Trinity does not associate itself with,
adopt or endorse any of the opinions or views expressed in
the selected songs.

THE EXAM AT A GLANCE

In your exam you will perform a set of three songs and one of the session skills assessments. You can choose the order of your set list.

SONG 1

Choose a song from this book.

SONG 2

Choose *either* a different song from this book
or a song from the list of additional Trinity Rock & Pop arrangements, available at trinityrock.com
or a song you have chosen yourself: this could be your own cover version or a song that you have written. It should be at the same level as the songs in this book and match the parameters at trinityrock.com

SONG 3: TECHNICAL FOCUS

Song 3 is designed to help you develop specific and relevant techniques in performance. Choose one of the technical focus songs from this book, which cover two specific technical elements.

SESSION SKILLS

Choose *either* **playback** *or* **improvising**.

Session skills are an essential part of every Rock & Pop exam. They are designed to help you develop the techniques music industry performers need.

Sample tests are available in our *Session Skills* books and free examples can be downloaded from trinityrock.com

ACCESS ALL AREAS

GET THE FULL ROCK & POP EXPERIENCE ONLINE AT TRINITYROCK.COM

We have created a range of digital resources to support your learning and give you insider information from the music industry, available online. You will find support, advice and digital content on:

- Songs, performance and technique
- Session skills
- The music industry

You can access tips and tricks from industry professionals featuring:

- Bite-sized videos that include tips from professional musicians on techniques used in the songs
- 'Producer's notes' on the tracks, to increase your knowledge of rock and pop
- Blog posts on performance tips, musical styles, developing technique and advice from the music industry

JOIN US ONLINE AT:

 /TRINITYROCKANDPOP    @TRINITY_ROCK    /TRINITYROCKANDPOP   and at **TRINITYROCK.COM**

CONTENTS

THE AUDIO

Professional demo & backing
tracks can be downloaded free,
see inside cover for details.

Music preparation and book layout by Andrew Skirrow for Camden Music Services
Music consultants: Nick Crispin, Chris Walters, Christopher Hussey, Donna Rudd
Drums recorded by Cab Grant and Jake Watson at AllStar Studios, Chelmsford
All other audio arranged, recorded & produced by Tom Fleming & Jeff Leach
Vocal arrangements by Jane Watkins & Christopher Hussey

Musicians
Bass: Tom Fleming, Ben Heartland
Drums: George Double
Guitar: Tom Fleming
Vocals: Brendan Reilly, Alison Symons, Emily Barden

YOUR
PAGE
NOTES

DON'T SPEAK NO DOUBT

WORDS AND MUSIC: ERIC STEFANI, GWEN STEFANI

SINGLE BY
No Doubt

ALBUM
Tragic Kingdom

B-SIDE
Greener Pastures

RELEASED
10 October 1995 (album)
15 April 1996 (single)

RECORDED
1994

LABEL
Interscope

WRITERS
Eric Stefani
Gwen Stefani

PRODUCER
Matthew Wilder

No Doubt formed in California in 1986 and released their self-titled debut album in 1992, by this point comprising Gwen Stefani (vocals), Tom Dumont (guitar), Tony Kanal (bass), Adrian Young (drums) and Eric Stefani (keys). Commercial success came with their third album, 1995's *Tragic Kingdom*.

Gwen Stefani wrote 'Don't Speak' with her brother Eric after the end of the singer's seven-year relationship with bandmate Kanal. Released as the third single from *Tragic Kingdom* six months after the album, it reached No. 1 in 12 countries including the UK, Australia and Canada. It was not released as a single in the US but topped the Hot 100 Airplay chart there for 16 weeks, the second longest period at the top in Billboard chart history. The Spanish guitar solo on 'Don't Speak' was spliced together from six different takes. Dumont said: 'I was thinking about how any true classical players would've hated the way I did it. I played it with a pick – a huge no-no.'

⚡ PERFORMANCE TIPS

This song begins with the note F over a C minor chord, which will need careful pitching. Other pitching challenges include many accidentals, the result of modulations which are not written in the key signature, so take care to observe all the sharps and flats. The chorus (bar 15) has a new feel, so sing more powerfully here. Note that in the second verse, a louder dynamic is introduced at the end of bar 26, which doesn't happen in the equivalent place the first time round.

DON'T SPEAK

WORDS AND MUSIC: ERIC STEFANI, GWEN STEFANI

SINGLE BY
Stevie Wonder

ALBUM
Songs in the Key of Life

B-SIDE
You and I

RELEASED
**28 September 1976 (album)
November 1976 (single)**

RECORDED
**1974-1976
Crystal Sound, Hollywood California, USA
Record Plant, Los Angeles California, USA
Record Plant, Sausalito California, USA
The Hit Factory, New York City, New York, USA (album)**

LABEL
Tamla

WRITER
Stevie Wonder

PRODUCER
Stevie Wonder

I WISH
STEVIE WONDER

WORDS AND MUSIC: STEVIE WONDER

Stevie Wonder is one of the most remarkable figures in popular music. A child prodigy who was blind since birth, he mastered piano, harmonica and drums by the age of ten before being signed by Motown boss Berry Gordy, aged 11. Two years later he scored his first US No. 1 single, the first of many hits, and went on to write, perform and produce a number of classic albums.

'I Wish' was the first single to be released from Wonder's 1976 self-produced double album *Songs in the Key of Life*, a commercial and critical hit and the third album in Billboard chart history to debut at No. 1. Wonder came up with 'I Wish' after attending a Motown company picnic in the summer of 76, an afternoon involving games that reminded him of his childhood. 'I had such a good time at the picnic that I went to Crystal Recording Studio right afterward and the vibe came right to my mind,' he said. The song was Wonder's fifth No. 1 in America and earned him a Grammy Award for Best Male R&B Vocal Performance. The bouncy, infectious bass line was played by Nathan Watts, who played with Wonder for the first time on the album and has done so on almost every one of his subsequent albums, as well as serving as his musical director.

⚡ PERFORMANCE TIPS

This soul-funk classic is full of typical Stevie Wonder vocal techniques, including staccato, syncopation, blue notes (the use of both G flat and G natural – make sure you note which is which!) and agility on semiquaver fills, for example at bar 19. The sum total of these features should be the joyful, energetic style that Wonder made his own. In bars 37-40 you are in rhythmic unison with the backing track, so take extra care with your accuracy here.

I WISH

WORDS AND MUSIC: STEVIE WONDER

Looking back on when I was a lit-tle nap-py-head-ed boy,

then my on-ly wor-ry was, for Christ-mas what would be___ my toy.

21. Greet-ed at___ the back door with, "Thought I told___ you not to go___ out-side?"___

23. ___ Try-ing your best to bring the

26. wa-ter to___ your eyes,___ think-ing it might stop her from

28. whip-ping your___ be-hind.___ I wish those days could_____

days could___ come back once more. Why did those days ev-

-er have to go? I wish those days could___ come back___ once more. Why did those

days___ ev - er___ have to go?

YOUR
PAGE
NOTES

IT'S TOO LATE
CAROLE KING

WORDS AND MUSIC: CAROLE KING, TONI STERN

SINGLE BY
Carole King

ALBUM
Tapestry

B-SIDE
I Feel the Earth Move

RELEASED
10 February 1971 (album)
April 1971 (single)

RECORDED
January 1971
A&M Recording Studios
Los Angeles, California
USA

LABEL
Ode Records

WRITERS
Carole King
Toni Stern

PRODUCER
Lou Adler

American singer, pianist and songwriter Carole King was born in Brooklyn, New York, and first found success penning songs in partnership with Gerry Goffin for various artists, including the US No. 1s 'Will You Love Me Tomorrow', 'Take Good Care of My Baby' and 'The Loco-Motion'. Her debut solo hit was 1962's 'It Might as Well Rain Until September' and her first solo album was released in 1970.

'It's Too Late' was released as a double A-side single with the song 'I Feel the Earth Move', both taken from Carole King's second album, 1971's *Tapestry*. It reached No. 6 in the UK and topped the US chart for five weeks, where two weeks later James Taylor's cover version of King's 'You've Got a Friend' (also from Tapestry) hit No. 1. The album itself spent 15 consecutive weeks at No. 1, still the longest unbroken run at the top for a female solo artist in the US. It went on to become one of the best-selling albums in music history, with sales of over 25 million copies. 'It's Too Late' won King a Grammy for Record of the Year in 1972, at the same time 'You've Got a Friend' won for Song of the Year and *Tapestry* for both Album of the Year and Best Female Pop Vocal Performance.

⚡ PERFORMANCE TIPS

This singer-songwriter classic features a clear message and natural, intuitive phrasing. The challenge is to sing it with honest, unaffected expression. Look out for occasional blue notes, for example the F natural in bar 9, and note how the chorus requires a stronger sound (for example in the pick-up to bar 13) before subsiding back into the softer sound of the verse (for example, the pick-up to bar 25).

IT'S TOO LATE

WORDS AND MUSIC: CAROLE KING, TONI STERN

Stayed in bed all morn-ing just to pass the time.___

There's some-thing wrong here there can be no de-ny - ing. One of us___ is chang-ing or

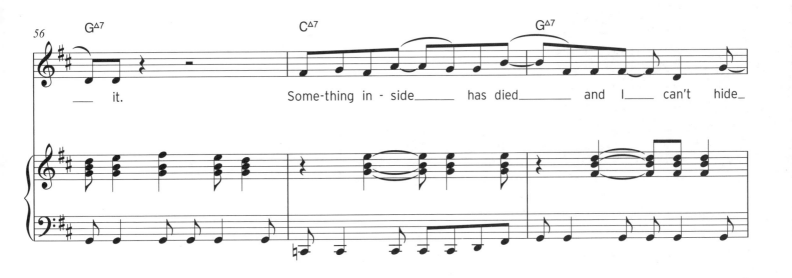

SINGLE BY
Dusty Springfield

ALBUM
Dusty in Memphis

B-SIDE
Just a Little Lovin'

RELEASED
8 November 1968

RECORDED
**September 1968,
American Studios,
Memphis, Tennessee,
USA**

LABEL
Atlantic

WRITERS
**John Hurley
Ronnie Wilkins**

PRODUCERS
**Jerry Wexler
Tom Dowd
Arif Mardin**

TECHNICAL FOCUS

SON OF A PREACHER MAN DUSTY SPRINGFIELD

WORDS AND MUSIC: JOHN HURLEY, RONNIE WILKINS

Hailed as one of the finest female singers Britain has ever produced, London-born Dusty Springfield scored a string of hits throughout the 60s, including 'I Only Want to Be with You', 'I Just Don't Know What to Do with Myself' and 'You Don't Have to Say You Love Me'. She found a new audience in the 80s thanks to her No. 2 hit with the Pet Shop Boys, 'What Have I Done to Deserve This?'.

Often ranked among the greatest albums ever made, Springfield's fifth album, 1969's *Dusty in Memphis*, was a commercial failure on its release. This is all the more surprising considering that it was released on the back of one of the all-time soul classics, 'Son of a Preacher Man', her tenth top-ten hit in the UK and third in the US. Recorded in Memphis with legendary producers Jerry Wexler, Arif Mardin and Tom Dowd, it features backing vocals by The Sweet Inspirations, the all-female quartet who can also be heard on such classics as Jimi Hendrix's 'Burning of the Midnight Lamp', Van Morrison's 'Brown Eyed Girl' and Aretha Franklin's 'Chain of Fools'. The song was originally offered to Aretha, who initially turned it down, but then recorded a version in 1970. The Dusty original was later memorably featured in Quentin Tarantino's 1994 film, *Pulp Fiction*.

TECHNICAL FOCUS

Two technical focus elements are featured in this song:

- Diction
- Pitching

This laid-back soul standard has a strong emphasis on storytelling, and the lyrics are conversational throughout, requiring clear **diction** despite the relaxed, conversational feel. There are lots of accidentals to look out for, many of them blue notes, which presents a challenge for **pitching**. As with the diction, precision is vital here, but this should be balanced with the need for a feeling of freedom in the delivery of this song.

SON OF A PREACHER MAN

WORDS AND MUSIC:
JOHN HURLEY, RONNIE WILKINS

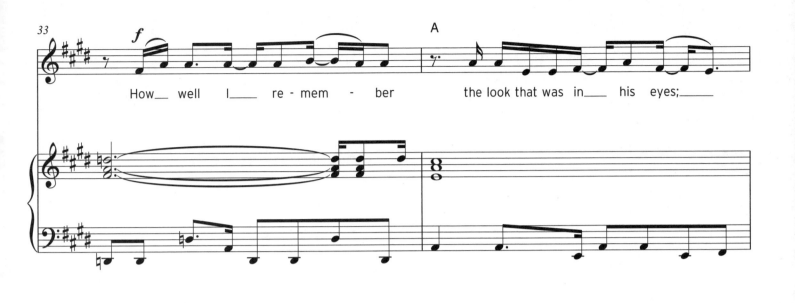

How__ well I__ re - mem - ber the look that was in__ his eyes;__

steal-ing kiss-es from me__ on the sly.__ Ta-king time to make__ time;

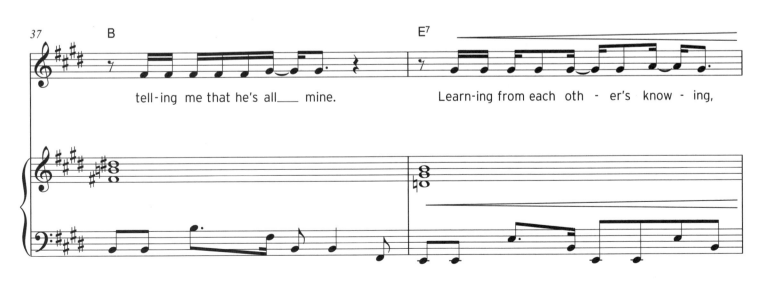

tell-ing me that he's all__ mine. Learn-ing from each oth - er's know - ing,

SINGLE BY
Natalie Imbruglia

ALBUM
Left of the Middle

RELEASED
24 November 1997

RECORDED
1997

LABEL
RCA Records

WRITERS
Anne Preven
Phil Thornalley
Scott Cutle

PRODUCERS
Matt Bronleewe
Mark Goldenberg
Phil Thornalley
Andy Wright
Gareth Parton
Nigel Godrich

TORN
NATALIE IMBRUGLIA

WORDS AND MUSIC: PHIL THORNALLEY, SCOTT CUTLER
ANNE PREVIN

Natalie Imbruglia is an Australian singer and actress who first found fame as a star of the long-running TV soap opera *Neighbours*. Her pop career launched in 1997 with the immediate international hit of her debut single 'Torn' and the success of its parent album *Left of the Middle*.

The song 'Torn' was originally released by the American rock band Ednaswap, and was written by the group's singer Anne Preven and its guitarist Scott Cutler along with English songwriter and producer Phil Thornalley (whose hit production credits include Prefab Sprout's 'When Love Breaks Down' and The Cure's 'The Lovecats', on which he also played the famous double bass part). Thornalley also produced the song for Ednaswap, though it made little impact when released as a single in 1995. Thornalley brought the song to Imbruglia two years later when working on her debut album, and 'Torn', produced by Thornalley and mixed by Radiohead producer Nigel Godrich, became a huge worldwide hit that achieved top five in most major countries. 'Torn' also topped the US airplay chart for 11 consecutive weeks.

 ## PERFORMANCE TIPS

This song makes a big feature of semiquaver-based syncopation – a subtle rhythmic displacement that characterises many of its phrases. The challenge is to stay close to the notated rhythms while maintaining a feeling of freedom in the phrasing. Look out for the B flats in bars 15 and 17 – these are blue notes and should create an expressive dissonance if pitched correctly.

TORN

WORDS AND MUSIC:
PHIL THORNALLEY, SCOTT CUTLER AND ANNE PREVIN

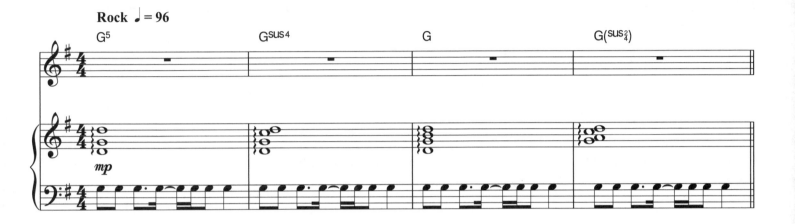

I thought I saw a man brought to life;

he was warm, he came a-round, and he was dig-

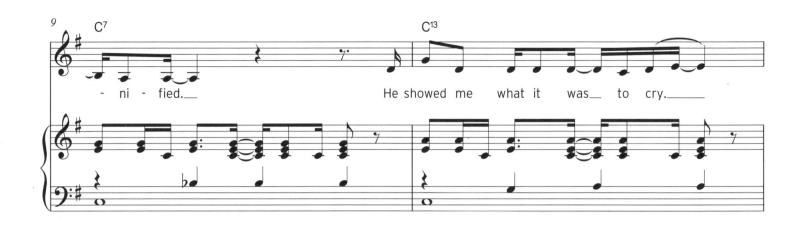

-ni-fied.___ He showed me what it was___ to cry.___

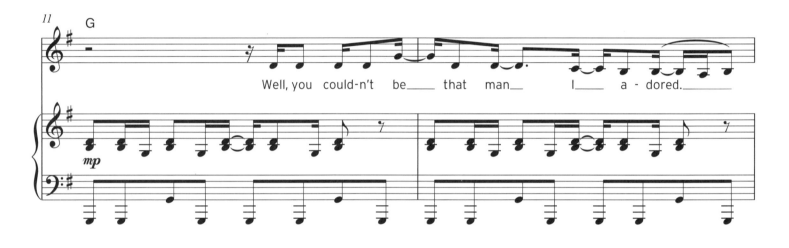

Well, you could-n't be___ that man___ I___ a - dored.___

You don't seem to know,___ don't seem to care___ what your

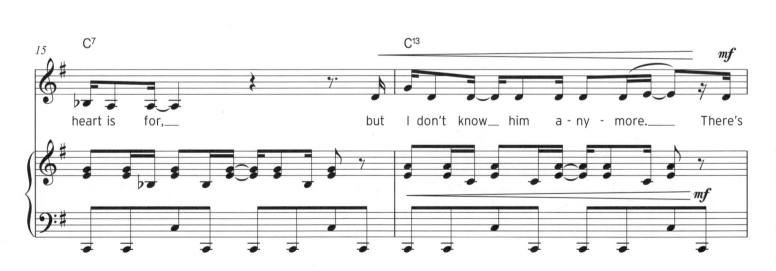

heart is for,___ but I don't know___ him a - ny - more.___ There's

YOUR
PAGE
NOTES

YOUR
PAGE
NOTES

TECHNICAL FOCUS

THE FIRST TIME EVER I SAW YOUR FACE ROBERTA FLACK

WORDS AND MUSIC: EWAN MACCOLL

SINGLE BY
Roberta Flack

ALBUM
First Take

B-SIDE
Trade Winds

RELEASED
20 June 1969 (album)
7 March 1972 (single)

RECORDED
24-26 February 1969
Atlantic Studios
New York City
New York, USA

LABEL
Atlantic

WRITER
Ewan MacColl

PRODUCER
Joel Dorn

North Carolina-born Roberta Flack grew up wanting to be a classical concert pianist before being hired to sing and play piano regularly at a jazz club in Washington DC. With a vast repertoire of some 600 songs and a building reputation garnered by her mesmerising late-night performances, she signed to Atlantic Records in 1969.

English Folk singer Ewan MacColl wrote 'The First Time Ever I Saw Your Face' in 1957 for his then lover and future wife Peggy Seeger. It was picked up by folk groups in the 1960s such as The Kingston Trio, Peter Paul & Mary and The Brothers Four, who all recorded versions. Flack recorded her slowed-down interpretation for her 1969 debut album *First Take*, though it would be almost three years before both would impact commercially after Clint Eastwood used the song in his hit 1971 directorial debut film *Play Misty for Me*. It subsequently topped the US singles chart for six weeks and helped propel her debut album to the top spot. The song went on to win Grammy Awards in 1973 for the coveted Song of the Year and Record of the Year, beating Don McLean's 'American Pie' in both categories. Many artists have since covered this classic love song, from Elvis Presley and Isaac Hayes to Johnny Cash and George Michael.

TECHNICAL FOCUS

Two technical focus elements are featured in this song:

- Breathing
- Diminuendos

This song features some very long phrases, which will require good control of **breathing** if they are to be sustained for their full duration. Many of the phrases end with long, drawn-out **diminuendos**, which should be as evenly gradated as possible. And of course, these technical points are in the service of a beautiful and expressive melody, the communication of which should be your top priority.

THE FIRST TIME EVER I SAW YOUR FACE

WORDS AND MUSIC: EWAN MACCOLL

and the stars_____ were the gifts you gave_____ to_

_the dark_____ and the end-less skies,_____ my love, to_

_____ the dark_____ and the end of the skies._____

And the first_ time_____ ev-er I kissed_____ your

was there_____ at my_ com-mand, my love.

The first_ time_____ ev-er I saw_____

your face, your face,

your face,_____ your face._____

SINGLE BY
Lana Del Rey

ALBUM
Born to Die

B-SIDE
Blue Jeans

RELEASED
7 October 2011

RECORDED
**2011
BMG Studios, New York
City, New York, USA**

LABEL
**Stranger Records
Interscope
Polydor**

WRITERS
**Lana Del Rey
Justin Parker**

PRODUCER
Robopop

VIDEO GAMES
LANA DEL REY

WORDS AND MUSIC: LANA DEL REY, JUSTIN PARKER

Please note: This song contains subject matter that some might find inappropriate for younger learners. Please refer to the Parental and Teacher Guidance at the beginning of this book for more information.

Born Elizabeth Grant, Lana Del Rey is a singer and songwriter from New York who found international fame with her second album, 2012's *Born to Die*, which topped the charts in ten countries including the UK. It was the year's fifth best-selling album worldwide with sales of over 3.4 million copies.

'Video Games' was first released to the internet on 29 June 2011, accompanied by a video Del Rey made herself using a webcam and footage taken from YouTube. It became a viral sensation and subsequently viewed more than 127 million times, leading to her signing a major label deal for her album, *Born to Die*. Del Rey co-wrote the song with English composer Justin Parker, who collaborated on five of the album's songs including the title track, released as its second single. 'Video Games' was a big international hit, reaching the top ten in 14 countries. It earned Del Rey an Ivor Novello Award for Best Contemporary Song, while NME named it Best Track of the Year. The romantic melancholia encapsulated in the song led Del Rey to comment: 'It's just really sad, it's myself in song form.'

⚡ PERFORMANCE TIPS

This song starts low in the chest voice at a quiet dynamic, requiring an intensity of tone to overcome the difficulties of register. The song is all about expression, and you'll need a cold composure to deliver its ambiguous message effectively. Take care to navigate the larger intervals without swooping too much, and pitch the first note of bar 24 carefully, as this note is not part of the chord.

VIDEO GAMES

WORDS AND MUSIC:
LANA DEL REY, JUSTIN PARKER

Swing-ing in the back-yard, pull up in your fast car, whis-tl-ing my name.

O-pen up a beer, and you say get o-ver here and play a vid-e-o game.___ I'm

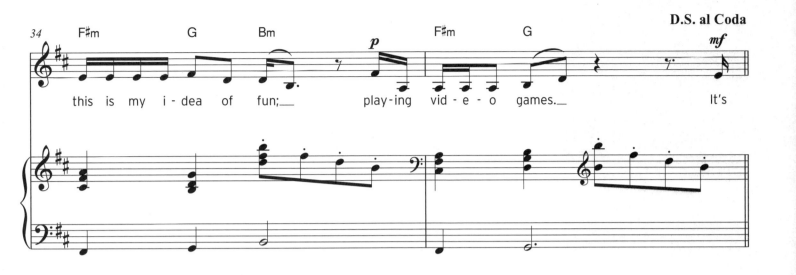

this is my i - dea of fun;___ play-ing vid - e - o games.___ It's

Coda

do.___ Mm._____ Now you

do,___ now, you do, now, you do.___

SINGLE BY
Paul Weller

ALBUM
Stanley Road

B-SIDE
**My Whole World is
Falling Down**

A Year Late

Woodcutter's Son

RELEASED
**7 June 1995 (album)
10 July 1995 (single)**

RECORDED
**1994
The Manor Studios
Oxfordshire, England**

LABEL
Go! Discs

WRITER
Paul Weller

PRODUCERS
**Paul Weller
Brendan Lynch**

TECHNICAL FOCUS

YOU DO SOMETHING TO ME PAUL WELLER

WORDS AND MUSIC: PAUL WELLER

Paul Weller is an English singer-songwriter whose first band The Jam had 18 consecutive top-40 singles in the UK between 1977 and 1982 (four of them No. 1s). Following his second band, The Style Council (1983–89), he launched a successful solo career in the 90s that has yielded 16 top-10 albums (four of them No. 1s).

'You Do Something to Me' was the third single released from Weller's third solo album, 1995's *Stanley Road*, his first No. 1 album in the UK and to date his biggest selling. In 2008 Weller performed 'You Do Something to Me' as a duet with Adele (who cites Weller as an influence) for a BBC 6 Music live session, and the following year Adele presented him with his third Best British Male Brit Award. Weller was also honoured by the Brits in 2006 for his Outstanding Contribution to Music, previous recipients of which include David Bowie, U2, Elton John, Queen and The Beatles.

TECHNICAL FOCUS

Two technical focus elements are featured in this song:

- Decorated melodic line
- Dynamics

This song features a highly **decorated melodic line**. Observe the notation carefully and listen closely to the performance track – these will help you to recreate all the detail in the phrases, which is an important part of this vocal style. There is great contrast in the **dynamics**, from the soft start to the louder chorus at bar 21. You'll need to find an intensity in the softer sound and maintain a full tone at the louder end, avoiding shouting.

TECHNICAL FOCUS

YOU DO SOMETHING TO ME

WORDS AND MUSIC: PAUL WELLER

just to___ get close___ to, just close e-nough___ to tell you that_____ you do___ some-thing to me,_____ some-thing deep in - side.

CHOOSING SONGS FOR YOUR EXAM

SONG 1

Choose a song from this book.

SONG 2

Choose a song which is:

Either a different song from this book

or from the list of additional Trinity Rock & Pop arrangements, available at trinityrock.com

or from a printed or online source

or your own arrangement

or a song that you have written yourself

You can perform Song 2 unaccompanied or with a backing track (minus the voice). If you like, you can create a backing track yourself (or with friends), include a live self-played accompaniment on any instrument, or be accompanied live by another musician.

The level of difficulty and length of the song should be similar to the songs in this book and match the parameters available at trinityrock.com

When choosing a song, think about:

- Does it work for my voice?

- Are there any technical elements that are too difficult for me? (If so, perhaps save it for when you do the next grade)

- Do I enjoy singing it?

- Does it work with my other songs to create a good set list?

SONG 3: TECHNICAL FOCUS

Song 3 is designed to help you develop specific and relevant techniques in performance. Choose one of the technical focus songs from this book, which cover two specific technical elements.

SHEET MUSIC

If your choice for Song 2 is not from this book, you must provide the examiner with a photocopy. The title, writers of the song and your name should be on the sheet music. You must also bring an original copy of the book, or a download version with proof of purchase, for each song that you perform in the exam.

Your music can be:

- A lead sheet with lyrics, chords and melody line

- A chord chart with lyrics

- A full score using conventional staff notation

SINGING WITH BACKING TRACKS

All your backing tracks can be downloaded from soundwise.co.uk

- The backing tracks begin with a click track, which sets the tempo and helps you start accurately

- Be careful to balance the volume of the backing track against your voice

- Listen carefully to the backing track to ensure that you are singing in time

If you are creating your own backing track, here are some further tips:

- Make sure that the sound quality is of a good standard

- Think carefully about the instruments/sounds you are using on the backing track

- Avoid copying what you are singing in the exam on the backing track – it should support, not duplicate

- Do you need to include a click track at the beginning?

COPYRIGHT IN A SONG

If you are a singer, instrumentalist or songwriter it is important to know about copyright. When someone writes a song they automatically own the copyright (sometimes called 'the rights'). Copyright begins once a piece of music has been documented or recorded (eg by video, CD or score notation) and protects the interests of the creators. This means that others cannot copy it, sell it, make it available online or record it without the owner's permission or the appropriate licence.

COVER VERSIONS

- When an artist creates a new version of a song it is called a 'cover version'

- The majority of songwriters subscribe to licensing agencies, also known as 'collecting societies'. When a songwriter is a member of such an agency, the performing rights to their material are transferred to the agency (this includes cover versions of their songs)

- The agency works on the writer's behalf by issuing licences to performance venues, who report what songs have been played, which in turn means that the songwriter will receive a payment for any songs used

- You can create a cover version of a song and use it in an exam without needing a licence

There are different rules for broadcasting (eg TV, radio, internet), selling or copying (pressing CDs, DVDs etc), and for printed material, and the appropriate licences should be sought out.

YOUR
PAGE
NOTES

YOUR
PAGE
NOTES

YOUR
PAGE
NOTES